THE **CRAZY WORLD** OF

MARRIAGE

CARTOONS BY

*Bilstott*

**EXLEY**
NEW YORK • WATFORD, UK

**Other cartoon giftbooks in this series:**
The Crazy World of Cats (Bill Stott)
The Crazy World of Football (Bill Stott)
The Crazy World of Gardening (Bill Stott)
The Crazy World of Golf (Mike Scott)
The Crazy World of Housework (Bill Stott)
The Crazy World of Rugby (Bill Stott)
The Crazy World of Sex (Bill Stott)

First published in hardback in the USA in 1996 by Exley Giftbooks.
Published in Great Britain in 1996 by Exley Publications Ltd.

12   11   10   9   8

ISBN 1-85015-768-5

Printed in China.

Exley Publications Ltd, 16 Chalk Hill, Watford, Herts, WD19 4BG, United Kingdom.
Exley Publications LLC, 232 Madison Avenue, Suite 1409, NY 10016, USA.

"It might make the world go round but it doesn't make it any tidier!"

"Say you love me."

"You love me."

"You don't understand. I think Madonna's fantastic,
ultimately sexy, amazing – a goddess – but I married you."

"Sorry about that, Darling, I didn't want to miss the goal.
You were saying something about having an affair...?"

"Done? I haven't done anything!"

"We had this room on our first honeymoon ... Look, Paul, there's the very window-seat where you sang 'Will you love me tomorrow'?"

"Why am I on the floor? Last night I tied the duvet to my big toe to stop you stealing it all. You're stronger than I thought."

"Well, there's nothing on TV and I feel like a good laugh.
Why don't we get the wedding photos out?"

"I see he's got his Dad's hair..."

"And when he does come to the supermarket, he's no help."

"Right, I've got my eyes closed. I just hope you haven't bought anything exotic this time – I can't abide your showy presents."

"Ease off, Dennis – these people are going to think
we're not married."

"I'm just trying to imagine what you'll look like when you're 50, just in case I'm still married to you by then..."

"The TV is broken. What is it to be – an argument or an early night?"

"I hate it when they take up a sport to be near you
and turn out to be good at it."

"Okay, there's something wrong isn't there? I know the signs..."

"You're not going to be masterful, are you? You always put your back out when you're masterful."

"Furthermore I also promise to avoid such terms as
'the wife', 'her' or 'my better half'."

"I see the Framlinghams had another fight."

"For heaven's sake, how many times have I told you about calling me at work?"

"He thinks I love him for his come-to-bed eyes.
Actually I'm crazy about the way he can't put shelves up."

"Sorry Darling – you were saying something about
how I don't notice you any more...?"

"Aah! A stiff breeze, a willing boat and the woman I love...
Happy, Darling?"

"My but you're magnificent when you're angry!"

"I said 'Why don't you do something for me you haven't done in years?'
He tried a headstand..."

"Just because I can't remember what we were fighting about,
doesn't mean I've forgiven you..."

"And the Lord have mercy on your soul. Ooops, turned over two pages there!"

"You want something to drive him mad? The effect or the bill?"

"Of course I'd really like to make it legal, but how do we know
he's a real priest?"

"Casserole? Again?"

"Okay, a truck smashed into our bedroom. But admit it – just for a second you thought the earth moved!"

"It's over then?"

"Hey Doreen – the guy on this TV counselling show just took a call from some woman who claims she hasn't had a meaningful conversation with her husband in 16 years ... Doreen?"

"I know I said it
with music in Majorca;
but this is not Majorca,
I'm freezing and there's
a policeman coming."

"You may be a mediocre lover, but nobody scratches a back like you do!"

"I wish my folks were like yours and hated pop music..."

"Ok, ok, you win. Your paper-hanging is better than mine."

"Get back on your pedestal instantly, woman."

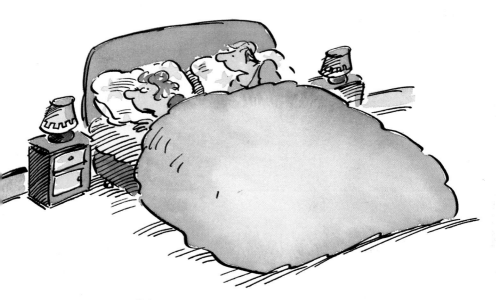

"It's my turn to have the headache."

"The old fool insisted on an anniversary waltz – and locked solid!"

"Of course the life insurance is paid up ... why?"

"You romantic old thing, you!"

"That ideal man you sorted out for me? It's worn out.
Got any more?"

"Yes, I've come back – but only because Hugo can't settle at my mother's."

"So this big mean-looking kid walks up and says 'Gimme the bag'.
And Gerry says 'Okay punk, beat it', didn't you Gerry?"

"Does the best man have the safety pin?"

"No problem, officer – it's just foreplay!"

"George! Stop telling my joke."

"Well I'm glad it's not <u>my</u> husband making a fool of himself!"

"And that's the Hopkinsons – they have some really good fights."

"No Dear ... Yes Dear ... Pick your mother up? Yes Dear...
Mow the lawn? Yes Dear... No Dear..."

"But I *do* still love you. It's just your clothes, politics, conversation and habits I want you to change."

"Wait a minute – we agreed. Tuesday is my day
to moan about the office!"

## Books in the "Crazy World" series

The Crazy World of Cats (Bill Stott)
The Crazy World of Football (Bill Stott)
The Crazy World of Gardening (Bill Stott)
The Crazy World of Golf (Mike Scott)
The Crazy World of Housework (Bill Stott)
The Crazy World of Marriage (Bill Stott)
The Crazy World of Rugby (Bill Stott)
The Crazy World of Sex (Bill Stott)

## Books in the "Fanatic's" series

The Fanatic's Guides are perfect presents for
everyone with a hobby that has got out of hand.
Over fifty hilarious colour cartoons by Roland Fiddy.

The Fanatic's Guide to Cats
The Fanatic's Guide to Computers
The Fanatic's Guide to Dads
The Fanatic's Guide to D.I.Y.
The Fanatic's Guide to Golf
The Fanatic's Guide to Husbands
The Fanatic's Guide to Love
The Fanatic's Guide to Sex

**Great Britain:** Order these super books from
your local bookseller or from Exley Publications Ltd,
16 Chalk Hill, Watford, Herts WD19 4BG.
(Please send £1.30 to cover postage and packing
on 1 book, £2.60 on 2 or more books.)